Around Hemel Hempstead In Camera

by Eve Davis

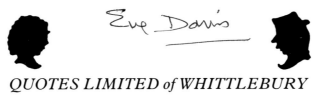

QUOTES LIMITED *of* WHITTLEBURY

MCMXCIII

Published by Quotes Limited in 1990
Whittlebury, Northants, England
and in this second impression in 1993

Typeset in Plantin by
Key Composition, Northampton, England

Pictures Lithographed by
South Midlands Lithoplates Limited, Luton, England

Printed by Busiprint Limited
Buckingham, England

Bound by Charles Letts Limited
Edinburgh, Scotland

ISBN 0 86023 383 9

Acknowledgements

I am grateful to the many people who have helped me with my requests for information and memorabilia. Every photograph and the smallest scrap of knowledge has helped to build up a picture of everyday living from years ago, and this in turn brings history to life! There is much precious material that has recently come to light; it has been difficult to know what to leave out.

Everything possible has been done to ensure accuracy and all copyright holders have been acknowledged where known. Nonetheless, if there are errors or omissions, they are mine. My special thanks go to Miss E. M. Dale for the interesting and informative talks we have had over many months, to the National Westminster Bank, Hemel Hempstead Local History and Records Society, the Hertfordshire Library Service, and the staff of the Hertfordshire Local Studies Collection, Hertford, and to the many people who have encouraged me to embark on this sequel to *Hemel Hempstead In Camera*.

I dedicate this book to my dear family and friends.

The History of Hemel Hempstead edited by Susan Yaxley (1973)

The Nicky Line James & Hedley Cannon (1977), Barracuda Books

The Book of Boxmoor Roger & Joan Hands and Eve Davis (1989), Barracuda Books

A History of Potten End Viviane J. M. Bryant (1986), Broxbourne Press

Kelly & Co Directory 1890, 1900, 1906, 1912, 1920, 1937

Hemel Hempstead and Dacorum town guides

Hemel Hempstead Gazette files

Key to Caption Credits

JA	Joan Allen	JBN	Mrs J.B. Newton
WA	W. Ambrose	JP	J. Picton
JC	J. Charman	MR	M. Roche
BC	Bert Cook	CS	C. Selden
DC	D. Coughtrey	JS	Jean Stevens
EMD	Miss E.M Dale	TT	Tina Thurlow
BE	B. Edwards	VW	Viv Weedon
EE	Eric Elborn	IW	I. Wells
DE	Mrs D. Embury	ARW	A.R. Wheeler
RF	R. Fonge	JWW	J.W. Winter
MG	M. Goddard	HHG	*Hemel Hempstead Gazette*
RG	Ron Green	HLS	Herts Library Service
BH	B. Hall	NWB	National Westminster Bank
LH	Mrs L. Ham	AC	Author's collection
JFH	J.F. Higham	LHS	Local History & Records
MH	Mrs M. Howard		Society
JM	J. Mann	CC	Cyril Collins
		FDG	F.D. Gardiner

FRONT COVER: This photograph was taken in 1902 when the landlord of the Whip and Collar was Samuel Newland. The present pub replaced this old building in 1936. (AC)

Hemel Hempstead has many neighbourhoods and villages surrounding it, all different but together contributing immeasurably to the town.

On the western side is *Adeyfield*, the first of the new neighbourhoods to be developed within the New Town plans of 1947 and also the largest. HM the Queen came to lay the foundation stone of St Barnabas Church just after her accession in 1952, a red letter day for the town.

Leverstock Green was a separate outlying hamlet, where brickmaking had developed into quite an important industry. It became an ecclesiastical parish in 1849 when the brand new Church of the Holy Trinity was consecrated.

In the 19th century, *Apsley* grew into an industrial area when the paper mills at Frogmore and Apsley opened, providing work for many. Kent's brush factory was another principal employer.

South-west of Hemel Hempstead is *Bovingdon*, where there has been a church since the Conquest. Nonetheless, until 1833, Bovingdon and Flaunden were served by Hemel Hempstead Parish. It has been said that services were only held when a visiting curate could be seen riding towards the village by the sexton, who climbed the church tower as look-out. The church bells were then rung to call villagers to prayer. Bovingdon had many cherry orchards and wheatfields and, at the only day school, children as young as three were taught straw plait. In 1941, Bovingdon grew in importance when an airfield was constructed, and US Flying Fortress bombers were flown in. It became a training base,

handed back to the RAF in 1946. Many locals will remember the 'circuits and bumps' training procedures that went on night after night. The airfield was closed in 1968, the site cleared and, after a time, part of the old airfield used for Sunday markets and banger racing. In March 1988 Mount Youth Prison was opened.

Down Box Lane, on the London-Aylesbury road, one mile north-west of Boxmoor, is *Winkwell* and *Bourne End* village, mentioned in documents of the 14th century. From Winkwell a steep road runs up to Pouchen End and on to Potten End.

Potten End village developed in the mid-19th century. It became a centre for market gardening. People who lived in the Frithsden and Potten End area were known as 'cherry pickers', because of the many fine orchards of black cherry trees.

Great Gaddesden, five miles north of Hemel Hempstead, stands on the Gade stream, which gives it its name. The Church of St John the Baptist is in the valley; there several monuments are dedicated to the Halsey family. Until recently, the, Halseys had lived in Gaddesden Place for almost 300 years. The 'golden parsonage' was built by a Thomas Halsey in 1705. He was Member of Parliament for Hertfordshire from 1688, a position held by his successors on and off, until Thomas F. Halsey was defeated by Nathaniel Micklem in the General Election of 1906. *Water End* is a small hamlet on the road between Great Gaddesden and Hemel Hempstead. For many years, local people have been campaigning for a by-pass as heavy traffic pounds the narrow but picturesque bridge.

Piccotts End has also opposed through traffic at rush hour and has achieved restrictions on road use.

In its time, *Hammerfield* has had many nicknames, among them Little Switzerland, Little Klondyke, the Deserted Village and Hammersplonk! In the 1880s William Cranstone, a well-known citizen of Hemel Hempstead, was the principal landowner. Many thousands of fir trees were planted, with plans for the construction of a few select properties. Builders moved in but went bankrupt before completing many houses, leaving them in various stages of construction. Several attempts were made to start small industries, including a boot factory, a mat factory and one which made croquet and cricket balls. In 1903, there were no street lamps, no post office or church, but by 1914 the village had all three. It was many years before the houses were completed, and steep gradients and unmade roads made transport difficult. A mission church dedicated to St Francis was in use in 1908 due to the generosity of Miss Carter of Park Hill. This is now the church hall. The new church, the design of which is partly based on the Church of St Mary of the Angels, Assisi, was opened on 5 July 1914 by the Bishop of St Albans.

The main part of *Boxmoor* in the 19th century was south of the London Road and Crouchfield was the area in and around St Johns Road. Boxmoor is fortunate to have its Trust lands and moors, dating back to Elizabethan times, especially when the canal and railway brought inevitable change. Boxmoor people had a wide choice of worship: there was Box Lane chapel founded in 1668, St Johns Church (which represented a separate parish in 1844), the Baptist church at Duckhall, and the Methodist chapel and Catholic church in the centre.

Industry included Fosters saw mills, a mineral water factory, an industrial brush factory, while some local families made a living from the many watercress beds which flourished in the spring-fed streams. Today, on a smaller scale, fresh local watercress is still available.

Within *Hemel Hempstead* itself, Marlowes is a long, winding road stretching from the Broadway by the entrance to Gadebridge Park to Moor End or 'funny roundabout', a name which may reflect an old family who were local landowners. Marlowes was originally a mixture of large houses, small shops and businesses of all kinds, open spaces and churches. The New Town brought dramatic change in 1947, when many old shops and other buildings were demolished. Forty years later, more changes take place. Since 1987 several 'new' buildings have vanished. The 1937 Post Office building has gone, to be replaced by a new block of buildings clad in dark glass. The post-war BP building, which straddled the road near the roundabout, has gone completely, as has the 'modern' multi-storey car park. Objections were raised when the Waggon & Horses came down, to be superseded by a new complex of shops and offices. Half of Marlowes as far as Tesco has been demolished, and large new buildings are emerging to include undercover shopping malls. A recent fire at Cheere House nurses' home caused extensive damage and now it awaits restoration while new hospital buildings are rising and the elderly from St Pauls have just been moved to new quarters at West Herts, in the spring of 1990.

As never before, change in Hemel Hempstead and its neighbouring areas accelerates, as yesterday becomes part of our history, even relatively recent years fade in the memory and the places and people of our past are put on record in books like this.

Some of the regulars of the Saracen's Head pose before their outing to the seaside in 1947: Jim and Fred Whiffen, Bob Chippin and his dad, Bill Smith, Arthur Smith, Bill Chiverton, Harry Edwards, Joe Davies, Claude Allard, Paddy Chevis and Cyril Latchford. The pub stood on the corner of Adeyfield Road, but was demolished when re-development took place. It was superseded by the New Venture, which opened in the Queens Square, Christmas 1952. (DE)

HM the Queen, shortly after her accession, came to Hemel Hempstead to lay the foundation stone of St Barnabas Church on 20 July 1952 in the Queens Square, Adeyfield. She was accompanied by the Bishop of St Albans. (AC)

Holy Trinity Church, Leverstock Green, was built in 1849, from local flints and pudding stones, and designed by R. & J. Brandon in 14th century style. The pulpit and font were donated by John Dickinson. (EMD)

Here c1905, the Baptist Chapel, Leverstock Green, was an offshoot of the parent chapel in Hemel Hempstead. It was demolished after finally being used as a Welfare Clinic. The first schoolhouse was erected in 1846 at the sole expense of the curate of Abbots Langley, Rev Edward Oswell, and cost him £200. The building was enlarged in 1857 and 1887. It was in use until a new school was built in 1931 at Pancake Lane. Many will remember Walter Ayre, Headmaster from 1922 until he retired in 1957. (WA)

This St Mary's Apsley Church group was taken around 1910. Only a few names are known, among them Collins, Hobday, Humphrey, K. Runham, May Walker, Jane Sells, Rodwell, Eva Sugars, Anne Hay, Winnie Dolt, Nellie Clifton, Lily Smith and, in the centre, Ref F. O. Houseman. (AC)

In this World War I victory procession outside the Salmon Public House, Apsley, this effort won an extra 5s in prize money. (JH)

Part of the original mill at John Dickinson's was simply called 'The Cottage'. Around 1927 it was extended to provide a new board room, directors' and visitors' dining rooms, a conference room and nurses' and first-aid room. (JP)

John Dickinson's 1951 entry for the town carnival included the telephone number, Boxmoor 124. This was an opportunity to promote the firm's paper products. All the participants were employees (the author is fourth from the left). The driver was Bob Coulson. (AC)

Boxmoor Band forms up in the grounds of Mr Butler's house (of Lambert & Butler fame) at the junction of Featherbed Lane and Bulstrode Lane in 1936. Top row from left: Sid Green, George Hunt, Bill Mills, George Scarfe, Jess Dealey, Bill Green, Eric Elborn, Alan Hollick, middle row: ?, Hosier, Basil Wicks, Bill Waite, Alf Cook, Frank Greenhill, Jack Antony, Les Waite, Harold Hunt, Bert Cross, Librarian; front row: Bert Mayo, Reg Sear, Stan Baines, Lol Sear, Bert Rolph, John Mew, Reg Austin, Bert Fowler in mufti. The uniforms cost £100, complete with caps! (EE)

G. B. Kent & Sons Ltd, brushmakers, came to Apsley End in 1905. They bought five acres and built houses and cottages for their employees. These buildings and gates disappeared when the site was re-developed, Kents built a smaller factory and the rest of the site became Texas Homecare & Bulk DIY, which opened in 1984. (AC)

Mr Arthur Hall's 'cycle workshop was next to the Bell at Two Waters. This young man, Alfred A. Green, aged 19, 'cycled from St Albans each day to work. This demonstration vehicle was possibly used for a carnival procession. Mr Green was proud of his own hand-built 'cycle, which had a double cross bar and 28" wheels, cost £9 19s 11d and was still in use, going strong until the 1960s. (RG)

Sarah Coughtrey's second-hand shop was along the London Road, near Two Waters. As was common in those days, the owners lived over the shop; the Coughtrey family later moved to be landlords of a pub and also had a scrap metal yard at the old Two Waters Mill. (TC)

This early picture of Two Waters School shows most girls in pinafores and boys wearing caps. Next to the school is the caretaker's house; c1900. (JP)

The camera looks towards Two Waters in the early 1950s. Many members of the Weston family had properties along this stretch of road, including Harold's billiard room, a well- known haunt for local lads, which had a fishing tackle shop at the front. Nearby was 'Roe' Weston's bakery. (AC)

Pupils and staff of the Central School, Two Waters in 1924: back row from left: Herring, ?, L. Picton, ?, ?, Corr?, ?, Snuggs, Rogers, Meadows, Hall, Lawrence, Stainforth, F. Lee, Frazer, Scott, Hooley, Cato, Skeets, Orchard; second row: Jennings, G. Fells, Bill (Chinny) Groom, Masters, Mead?, Cowley, E. Hannant, G. Picton, Rodwell, Roland Clark, Surridge, Dickie Bird, B. Brook, Les Boarder, Waterton, ?, Jim Harris, Breed, Storrow, H. Toovey; third row: Kit Gurney, Alice Rogers, Lily Squires, ?, Vera Hobday, ?, Elsie Akery, Beatrice January, Ivy Charge, Joyce Morton, Fred Tyres, Alex Pearce, ?, Shepherd, ?, Lila Pettitt, Vera Clark, Gladys Fowler, Nellie Strudwick, Vi Castle, Edie Hearn, Daisy Austin; fourth row: Kath Gower, Elsie Howe, Kitty Minks, Lily Halsey, Millicent Ling, Winnie Bates, Muriel Coxhill, Miss Badcock, Mr Warren (headmaster), Mr Inkster, Mrs Gregory, Edie Snoxall, Vida Foster, Vera Caffall, Mary Mason, Marjorie Carter, Tilly Saunders, Gladys Winters; short row: Win Geary, South, Kath Goff, Hilda Coker; front row: Mabel Attwood, ?, Edna Sanders, Surridge, Madge Thorne, Lily Puddephatt, Phil Squires, Nellie Ranscombe, Molly Cato, Win Henley. The photo was taken by Pattersons of Apsley. (MR)

LEFT: Mr John Mann and RIGHT: his family, outside his draper's shop at 419 London Road; his wife Mary, son John and one of his daughters, (Gwen or Olive). The Felden Dairy next door was absorbed to form Fisher, Hammond & Duck, which eventually became the Hygienic Dairies. The neighbour on the other side was the Oxford Brotherhood, a thriving Bible Class group for men, ably run by Miss Marnham. (JM)

This photo of the Boxmoor Boys' Brigade standing in front of the 'Boxmoor Colliery' has posed a problem. No documented evidence of a colliery in the area can be found, but further along on Roughdown Common was a chalk mine owned by more than one generation of the Glover family, which probably began around 1850. It contained a narrow gauge railway for the transport of chalk through its many passages. Instability became a problem and the entrances were sealed in 1916. An investigation and survey was carried out in 1971. This first aid demonstration was possibly an exercise in dealing with a 'colliery accident'.

Mrs Ada Edwards stands outside her home with her family — William, Dennis and in her arms Florence — around 1908. The 17th century moorman's cottage in London Road is a listed building. Mrs Edwards looked after many 'gentlemen of the road' in return for chopping wood and other menial tasks; she would give them a good dinner, fill up their billy-can with tea and, with a lump of fruit cake, send them on their way. She also sold sweets, lemonade and Boxmoor rock! This 'herdsman's cottage' is under threat to make way for the A41 by-pass. (BE)

Box Lane Congregational Chapel has a long past. It was erected about 1600. In the 19th century, when alterations were made, Roman remains were discovered. Over 350 years of worship came to an end when the Chapel finally closed its doors on 29 June 1969. This photograph was found among the papers of Mr Francis Moore, treasurer of the Chapel in 1913. It has now been changed to an attractive home. (IS)

St Lawrence Church, Bovingdon is well known for its avenue of yew trees. A church has been on this site for centuries, but the present building opened in 1846. Much of the money for its construction was provided by the Ryder family.
(AC)

The well in the centre of Bovingdon was built in 1881, in memory of Granville Dudley Ryder, Lord of the Manor, whose family lived at Westbrook Hay. A pond nearby had a habit of flooding from time to time during heavy rain. This area is known locally as Bovingdon Docks. The Bull, the Bell and the Wheatsheaf are Bovingdon's three pubs, all in the vicinity. (JL)

27

The VAD Herts/34 Detachment underwent a War Office Inspection in April 1939. They were formed in October 1938. Commandant was the Hon Mrs de Yarburgh Bateson; Asst Commandant, Mrs Beck; Medical Officer, Dr Gilbert Burnet. The inspection was carried out by Major W. Parsons RAMC, accompanied by Miss Tindall-Lucas, Asst County Controller for Herts. This photo was taken outside the Memorial Hall, Bovingdon. (HB)

Bourne End is within the boundary of the Borough of Hemel Hempstead, but was outside the area of the New Town Plan. The tiny Church of St John was erected as a chapel-of-ease in 1854. It became the parish church of Bourne End in 1913. The chancel and altar are dedicated to the memory of Edward Curtis' first wife, Elca Rose, who died at the early age of 24. (AC)

At Winkwell, three boundaries meet — Bovingdon, Northchurch & Hemel Hempstead. The Three Horseshoes has been nicknamed the Pier Hotel, possibly in connection with the swing-bridge alongside. Parts of the building date back to the 16th century. During the last world war paper money from different countries was pinned on the ceiling behind the main bar until it was completely covered. (EMD)

Pouchen End Cottages in the 1880s when Mr H. E. Dale was head gardener. Arum lilies were grown in large numbers and shipped to London. Just off the photo on the left was a windmill, used to pump water. (EMD)

There was a Red Lion pub on this site at Potten End in 1838. This photo shows the modern building erected in 1924. Lane's Nurseries owned many acres of land in the village and were the largest local employers. The Lanes' advertising board is to the left of the pub. The pond was not banked and heavy rain caused it to overflow into the small pond by Martin's Hedge. (VW)

Holy Trinity Chapel, Potten End, was provided by the generosity of Earl Brownlow and other subscribers. It was consecrated in 1868 and, for the first 30 years, it was ruled by three Berkhamsted rectors. All the seats, unlike those in most churches then, were free. It became the Parish Church in 1895 and was licensed for weddings as well as baptisms and funerals. (AC)

Potten End was fortunate to have a local transport service. B & B Bus Services stood for Bedford and Barnard or 'Bumps & Bruises'. It was quite common for passengers to get off and help push at times; no reductions in fares when this occurred! In the 1980s the business was taken over by Tates of Markyate. (VW)

The wooden barns on the left of this tranquil scene in Great Gaddesden were demolished in 1962 to make way for the car park to the Cock & Bottle pub. The Church of St John the Baptist dates from the 13th century. Several monuments there are dedicated to the Halsey family, who lived in nearby Gaddesden Place. (MG)

This large white house is called River View, is over 400 years old and has been the home of the Fowler family for more than a century. Mr J. Fowler took people in wagonettes to Boxmoor Station and brides to their weddings. Sylvia and Emmeline Panhkhurst were frequent visitors and a flag was flown from the chimney when they were in residence. The smaller timbered building is the oldest house in Water End at 500 years. (MG)

Charles Dickinson Waite was postmaster and beer retailer at Water End between 1895 and 1910. The buildings have been preserved and are almost the same today. The Post Office later became a saddlery, but is now a private house. Heavy through traffic is the main problem for residents of this pleasant and once tranquil hamlet. (MG)

Piccotts End School won the Davidson Cup for the first time when netball finals were played on the Salmon Meadow, Apsley, in April 1933. The team was — back row: Gladys Foster, Olive Ginger (teacher), Miss Foxall, Doris Baker, Nancy Perry; front: Jocelyn Vercoe, Dorothy Collier and Thora Dennis. (OM)

A rare photograph shows Piccotts End Church, before it became a private house. All Saints Church was built in 1907 with a legacy left by Nathaniel Wishart Robinson. One of the last curates in charge was Gilbert Wood; Arthur Snuggs played the organ. (WA)

After the Coronation celebrations of 1911 in the High Street, the shop signs under these decorations spelt out Bagnall & Oakley, drapers and milliners, where blouses in stock ranged from 1s 11½d to 35s, and Henry Anderson, hairdresser, tobacconist and seller of a large variety of fancy goods. Today Bagnall's is a dentist's surgery and the other shop, until recently a greengrocery, is now empty. (WA)

LEFT: The 3rd Boxmoor Troop of Scouts took part in the annual United Friendly Societies' demonstration in aid of the West Herts Hospital in 1923. The High Street has not changed much since those days. The outfitters sign SPQR stood for Small Profit Quick Returns. RIGHT: Local photographer F. Barrett Gardiner of 17 Alexandra Road, celebrated V-E Day with colourful decorations. Part of the shop was Betty Jean, ladies' and children's hairdresser. The photographic business was sold in 1952 when Mr Gardiner retired. (FDG)

There were many local names to jog the memory here in Bury Road in the 1950s. Smiths' furniture store, Oldfields, blacksmiths, Osborne & Tyres trade tobacconists, Bricketts' ironmongers, Paynes the sweep and Knight's chip shop. At the end of the road were the six Bells pub, the Star Brewery, with a fox on the weathervane, and Sid Williams' hairdressers and newsagents. Tucked around the corner were Stainforths and the Nags Head pub. (Herts Lib.S)

Bury Mill goes back to before the 17th century. In the mid-1930s a fire broke out one Sunday lunchtime in the upper floors of the old Mill, where Christmas decorations were made (it was known as the tinsel factory). The lower part of the building was used by Mr Howard of Howards Motors. During World War II employees were kept busy making army greatcoats. In the small building were the premises of Archie Windmill, a local speedway rider. (MH)

Bury Road was once the terminus for 'buses. Several routes used to be lined up here alongside the high brick wall of The Bury. Those were the days when conductors gave out punched 'bus tickets in a wide array of colours according to the price of the fare. (JFH)

Miss Foden's house and nursery were all decked out for Queen Victoria's Jubilee of 1897. In 1930, a sheaf of wedding flowers there cost 17s 6d + 1s 6d for ribbon. Two bridesmaids' posies of pink and cream roses were 12s 6d each, and buttonholes were 6d each. The property was later used by Brown & Merry, house agents, before being demolished to make way for a Jewish retirement home. (JP)

In the First World War, artillery troops, guns and carriages litter the fields of Handpost Farm, once the home of the Statty Fair. In the distance are the Parish Rooms and St Pauls Church, closed in 1961 and demolished; flats now occupy the site. The parish room became the headquarters of the Hemel Hempstead Conservative Association and was renamed Davidson House. (HHG)

Dacorum College now occupies this area of buildings and shops, then known as Cheapside (c1910). The Sebright Arms stood on the corner of Alma Road. Cheapside bakery later became Wadkins and Pellings was taken over by Lilian, hairdressers. The trees on the left were replaced by a parade of shops in the 1930s. (JW)

A happy group of ladies and children gather at the rear of the Salvation Army Citadel when it was in Marlowes. This was probably an afternoon Home League meeting in 1935. A few of the people in the photo are: Mrs Avery, Mrs Henden, Mrs Capel, Hall, Brigadier Stebbings, Mrs Peach, Newberry, Fountain , Mrs Marshall, Eva Pratt, Miss Rose Humblestone, Mrs Newton, Lil Bradding, Mrs Fowler, Mrs Cooley, Win Page, Mrs Collier, Rose Cheshire, Mrs Ethel Cook and her daughter, Joyce. (JWW)

Another once familiar shop in Marlowes, Raynes ladies' dress shop, opened in 1956 and closed in 1986 because of fast-rising rents. In 1956 the older buildings and shops were still standing on the other side of the road — Andrews, Wadkins and Humphreys. These were also soon to go as new shops took their place. (JBN)

LEFT: Not many will remember Cheere House looking like this, (c1950) on the corner of King Harry Lane & Hospital Lane. Formerly a convalescent home, then a nurses' home, it was later hidden from view when shops and offices were built along Marlowes. Hospital Lane was re-named Hillfield Road. RIGHT: More old shops along Marlowes: Bridge Street Domestic Electric, where most electrical items could be found; Attwoods and cycles always went together and John Wallis the cleaners, approximately where Sainsbury's now stands. (HH)

The procession for the town's 1948 pageant arrives from the direction of the Plough and railway bridge in Marlowes. Mr S. Hancock was Henry VIII. The shops seen here include Moorecroft (greengrocer), Fortnum (butcher), Garments (grocer), Smiths (picture framer) and, tucked in just before the bridge, Harris (barber). On the right was Anderson & Woodman (by the bridge) a small shoe repair shop, a café and a row of cottages; the Waggon & Horses is just outside the picture. (HHG)

One of the most recent landmarks to go was the much-loved Waggon & Horses pub, demolished in March 1989 for a new Lakeside development. A small beer house kept by John Hoar in 1851 was first built on the site, but was later rebuilt on a much larger scale. It also had a large restaurant added on at the rear of the building and a play area for children. (CC)

Celebrations for Queen Victoria's Jubilee in 1897 at the Plough show the railway bridge and cottages leading up Marlowes to the town. The only traffic on the road then was an occasional horse and cart. (JA)

Lavers Wharf at Corner Hall in the 1950s; the business began in 1869 and, when the firm expanded, part of the wharf was filled in to allow for much-needed storage space. (EMD)

Riverside was the Moor End home of the Carey sisters, who were founder members of the Baptist Church at Two Waters. Their father, William Carey, was the first missionary of the new Baptist Missionary Society to go out to India. The house is marked on an 1898 OS map, but between that date and 1926 it had gone. (JS)

Heath Park Hotel was an elegant building in the Georgian style, on the corner of Cotterells and St Johns Road. Next to it, in complete contrast, is Boxmoor Hall, which looks older but was built in 1890, partly with funds from Boxmoor Trust, to be used as a recreational centre for local people. It became a magistrates' court for a time and is now an arts centre and crèche. (EMD)

LEFT: Mrs Clara Tovey and Mr Henry Jaquest, Pearly King & Queen of Tottenham, collected funds in World War II. This photo was taken in Station Road during Warship Week, 1941. (JBN) RIGHT: Steam railway enthusiasts gathered at Heath Park Halt, when a special day was arranged for the 11 May 1957 closing of the Midland Line; this is an 0-6-0 tender, Class 14C, number 43245. (BC)

It was a wintry wedding for Cub Master Bray and his bride, Miss Muriel Garner, at St John's Church in 1923. The District Commissioner, E. H. Lidderdale, and Assistant Scoutmaster Poulter attended, and some of the Wolf Cubs from the 3rd Boxmoor Troop formed a guard of honour. (RG)

The clergy with the choir of St John's Church included ladies c1923 — back row left to right: Les West, Maurice Snoxall, Ted Busby, Ernie Hannant, Eric Hannant, ?; next row includes Clive Shuff, Dennis Gower, Chris Humphrey, Sidney Smith, Mr Glover, Mr West, Mr Sid Pearman, Ted Edwards, Frank Badcock, Leslie Attwood, Mr Seabrook, Mr Mitchell-Innes, Mr Ayre, Mr Woodman, sidesman; ladies' row: Molly S., Barbara Collard, Miss Greenhill, Miss Evitts, Mr Douglas Jones (organist), Rev Smith-Cranmore, Mr Bealy (Curate), Miss Elsie Badcock, Miss Hawkins, Kate B., Miss Mary England; front row: ?, Dennis Clarke, Les Johnson, Jack Cato, ?, Ted Picton, Laurie Jenkins, Claude Colman, Wilfred Emmines. (AC)

Maypole dancers at Churchill Grounds in the 1930s: Beryl Bates, Marjorie Goodman, Phyllis Butterfield, Doris Beckwith, Gwen West, Joyce Smith, Alice Austin, Rene Tomlin, Vera Tomlin, Lily Whitehouse, Marjorie Moorecroft, Marie Hall, Kathleen Marshall, Zena Milsom, and the boys in the centre — Reg Austin and Peter Moorecroft. (LH)

Herts/92 Red Cross Detachment had their headquarters at Churchill in the 1940s, manned twenty-four hours a day. Medical Officer Dr Garry trained the members. Miss M. Saunders, Win Jordan, Elsie Williams, Miss M. Dale, Ida Williams and Mrs Gregson are some of the people in this photo. (EMD)

Victory celebrations in 1945 here saw the Boxmoor Company of the Boys' Brigade parade on the Moor opposite 'Pansy Potters' shop. The boys met in Brockman Hall behind Duckhall Chapel. Mace Bearer: Trevor Fuller; some of the others taking part were: Brian Lockyer, Tommy Cave, B. Ashby, Reg Palmer, Doug Hearn, Norman Parsons, Peter Davis, Arthur Cross, Colin McDonald, Jack Rands and Captain Smith at the rear. (AC)

South Hall in Heath Lane about 1912 belonged to the Burbeck family and was later taken over as a girls' school. The workmen are, from the left: Reg Hoar, Sid Vercoe, Mont Hoar, Jack Wells, Billy Cox, George Groom, Harry Williams, Sear, Lewis Latchford, Billy French, on the steps, Harry Pipkin & Alfred Selden. The dog's name was Gyp. The extra-long ladders were made in the ballroom by hand by Billy Cox, carpenter, using only hammer, chisel and a plane. (CS)

LEFT: Rev Smith-Cranmore, Vicar of St John's from 1917 to 1927; Mr Fletcher, the Vicar and the people of Boxmoor worked hard to raise funds for the new church hall. The Parish Rooms in Horsecroft Road (built with money given by Rev Ritchings) were sold to help. (EMD) RIGHT: Mr Badcock with his daughter, Dorothy, stands outside his house adjoining St John's School, with (possibly) Elsie Badcock with the bicycle. He was headmaster at the school from 1877-1917. (AC)

The staff of St John's School, Boxmoor in 1908 included — back row: Mr Turner, Mr Jenkins, Miss Brunton, Miss Turner; front row: Miss England, Miss Carter (head teacher), Mr Badcock (headmaster), Elsie Badcock. Miss Mary England was a monitress and hoped to go on to be a teacher, but instead she spent all her working life at Dickinson's. (JP)

Boxmoor Cricket Club played opposite the Steamcoach on a piece of moor called The Oval. This is a photo of the team in 1939 — back row from left: Arthur Glover, Charlie Coulson, C. Bradbury, Puddephatt, Archie Trott, Youdes, Inky Perry?; front row: Charlie Plummer, Jim Hosier, Harold Garment, Eric Bindoff, Bob Poulter, Lal Tomlin. (AC)

Staff stand proudly outside the new Hemel Hempstead Post Office in Horsecroft Road in 1906. The low building behind was the sorting office, conveniently sited near the town's Boxmoor railway station. These post office rooms were used by the community for jumble sales, club meetings and wedding receptions, when larger sorting offices were opened in the town centre. Foster Road is the name of the narrow road, all that is left to remind us of the sawmills that once stood in Kingsland Road. (AC)

Everyone knew 'Waxy Bates', the local cobbler, famous for always wearing a bowler, so old it had gone green with age. This is an old photo of the Bates family — back row from left: Margaret Bates, who married Henry Hill; Edie, wife of George (Waxy) Bates; Ann Bates, who married Joe Collier; front row: Polly Bates married Charlie Andrews, the old couple, Mr & Mrs Bates, lived in Horsecroft Road where Waxy had his business for a while, until he moved to his shop on the corner of Puller Road and St John's Road around 1912. The last lady in the photograph is uncertain but may be Emm Bates? (MP)

68

This house in St John's Road, and on the corner of Cowper Road, was called The Laurels and was owned by the Green family. Westminster Bank opened the sub-branch there in July 1937. Previously bank business was done in a shop across the road in what is now Milnes DIY shop. The open space later became a greengrocery run by 'Nodder' Crawley. Locals will remember it as 'Bindoffs'; Eric and Vi ran the shop for many years. Today it is still a greengrocery called 'Pippins'. (NWB)

Cowper Road infant school in 1924 included back row from left: Sid Townsend, Raymond England, Dorothy Pigg, ?, Winnie Cox, Agnes Weston, Dennis Bateman, Knight; middle row: Marie Hall, Ron Lee, Marjorie Goodman, Lilly Whitehouse, Cyril Ambrose, Dorothy South, Winnie Sherfield, ?, ?, Doris Phipps, Douglas Wright; front row: Doris Beckwith, Bob Squires, Nellie Newton, Dennis Greenhill, Lucy Bates, Peter Cato, Gladys Castle, Winnie Burke, Marie Hall. In the background can be seen a small boy and Mr Cox, a local milkman. (LH)

Two well-known past local residents — LEFT: Mr Marshall, the chemist at the bottom of Cowper Road until the late 1930s, kept bees and was famous for his many patent medicines, made on the premises. His cough cure was thought to be the best for miles around. (EMD) RIGHT: Miss E. M. Salisbury, artist and historian, lived in Box Lane. This snap was taken by her painting companion in Anchor Lane, when traffic was almost non-existent. She was a keen gardener and at 94 was still to be seen shopping in the village. She died at 97 in October 1980. (EMD)

Where Anchor Lane and St John's Road converge, this between-wars view shows the old buildings of Home Farm dairy, the Barn and Ranscombes' bakery. Reynolds bought the dairy in 1902; the last owner was Bob or 'Bonny' Proctor. The buildings were demolished when the roads were widened. Recently a block of three new housesd have been built on this corner. (EMD)

This beer house in Anchor Lane shows the landlord, William Todd and his family outside in 1902. The little girl on the right is Ethel May South when she was about eight years old. The building was demolished for re-development and a new pub of the same name built on the corner of Anchor Lane and the new Beechfield Road in the early 1950s.
(IW)

Hammerfield has been known by many names, including Little Switzerland, the Deserted Village and 'Hammersplonk'. It was once an isolated spot. The new Church of St Francis was opened in July 1914, architect, Paul Waterhouse. (AC)

The original Church of St Francis dates back to 1908; before that services were held in one of the cottages — 7 Glenview Gardens. This building is now the church ha.l. A generous benefactress, Mrs Carter, distributed buns on St Francis's Day annually at the door of the Church. This tradition carried on until at least 1916. (HHG)

An early view of Hammerfield around 1910 demonstrates the steep gradient of the road; the baker's horse and cart had to be left at right angles for safety while deliveries were made. Later, the building on the extreme left became a post office. Sadly it had to close, but the grocery side is still much used. (JT)

Lockers Park School, established in 1874, stands in 23 acres of ground. Mr Percy Christopherson was headmaster when Lord Louis Mountbatten was a pupil there in 1910-1913. A close association grew between the school and St John's Church and, from 1874 to 1906, the boys and staff attended services at the Church until the school had its own chapel. The local postman found out to his cost that no whistling was allowed on the school premises when he walked up the long drive to deliver letters. (AC)

Chaulden House just before it was demolished; during the 1939/45 war it was used by the Ever-Ready battery firm for their workers. Single people lived in dormitories, and were ferried to and from work at Tottenham by the firms' own transport. The floods of 1947 caused many to be marooned in the house for several days. (AC)

This ornate water tower c1915, decorated with flints and shells, used to pump up water to Chaulden House. It was a well-known landmark for many years, partly destroyed by fire and finally demolished. A nearby boathouse also belonging to the Chaulden Estate was decorated in the same manner and had the jaw-bone of a whale as the entrance.

(AC)

Index to Illustrations